ESL ANIMALS 1
The Alphabet A to L

Student Reader
Student Workbook
Teacher Guide

Daisy A. Stocker M.Ed.
George A. Stocker D.D.S.

Learning English Curriculum

Copyright © 2023 ALL RIGHTS RESERVED.

You are permitted to print or photocopy as many copies as you need for your school. Online distribution is not permitted. Please contact us if you wish to teach online.

Re-Sales is not permitted.

Notice: Learning English Curriculum makes every reasonable effort to obtain from reliable sources accurate, complete, and timely information about the tests covered in this book. Nevertheless, changes can be made in the tests or the administration of the tests at any time and Learning English Curriculum makes no representation or warranty, either expressed or implied as to the accuracy, timeliness, or completeness of the information contained in this book. Learning English Curriculum make no representations or warranties of any kind, express or implied, about the completeness, accuracy, reliability, suitability or availability with respect to the information contained in this document for any purpose. Any reliance you place on such information is therefore strictly at your own risk.

The author(s) shall not be liable for any loss incurred as a consequence of the use and application, directly or indirectly, of any information presented in this work. Sold with the understanding, the author is not engaged in rendering professional services or advice. If advice or expert assistance is required, the services of a competent professional should be sought.

ISBN: 978-1-77245-405-5

Published by:
Learning English Curriculum
Visit us online
https://www.efl-esl.com

ESL ANIMALS 1
A TO L

STUDENT READER

This Student Reader is Ready to Use.

It is Part of our Colorful Conversational Series that Includes
a Student Reader, Workbook,
and a Teacher's Guide with Unit Tests and a Final Test.

In this Student Reader the children listen, gain understanding from the colorful pictures, identify beginning sounds from A to L, participate in role-plays and say what they would do if they were part of the story.

Teacher instructions are provided in small boxes on each page.

George and Daisy Stocker
Learning EnglishCurriculum
E-mail: **info@efl-esl.com**

ESL ANIMALS
A TO L

STUDENT READER

CONTENTS

			PAGES
Introduction			1
Chapter 1	Aa	George and Elizabeth	2-4
Chapter 2	Bb	baboons	5-6
Chapter 3	Cc	cat	7-9
Chapter 4	Dd	dinosaur	10
Chapter 5	Ee	elephant	11-12
Chapter 6	Ff	fish / frog	13-14
Chapter 7	Gg	goose / gander / gosling	15-17
Chapter 8	Hh	horse	18-20
Chapter 9	Ii	iguana	21-22
Chapter 10	Jj	jackal	23-24
Chapter 11	Kk	kids / kittens	25-27
Chapter 12	Ll	lions	28

ESL ANIMALS 1
STUDENT READER
CHAPTERS 1 to 12

This Student Reader is presented in a graphics novel format stressing listening, speaking, understanding, and phonics. It introduces the alphabet letters from A to L and associates them with animals, birds and food. It is designed for children aged 6 to 8 years who have matured past the need for reading readiness and fine motor control practice.

The children will see wild animals on a big screen. They'll interact with friendly animals.

The **Student Reader** can be used by many different classes as the children don't write in it. Teacher instructions are given in smaller print at the bottom of each page. The suggestions provide oral practice and enhance student understanding.

This Reader introduces the alphabet from A to L with pictures and simple dialogue for role-plays. The children are introduced to their teacher, a panda bear. He explains the names and sounds of the letters, using key words and animal pictures. The two storybook characters, George and Elizabeth, introduce themselves. They speak to the children in your class saying, "We have fun." They then invite everyone in the class to join their adventures. At the end of each chapter George and Elizabeth introduce the next lesson by talking about what they are going to do next.

The **Workbook** teaches printing between lines using key word examples. It provides the children with many opportunities to participate with the storybook characters. Teacher suggestions are provided in small print on each page. These guide the teacher in presenting the lessons in the best way.

Panda Bear, the teacher, names the letters and models what they say. The children have practice printing the letters and key words between the lines. Understanding of the key words is reinforced with colorful pictures.

The numbers are introduced with the oral counting of a series of pictures.

The **Teacher's Guide** includes **Tests** to be given after every fourth lesson and **Picture Bingo** games that review and reinforce the children's understanding of the materials taught. Detailed instructions for playing the game are provided in this Teacher's Guide

After introducing how to play Picture Bingo, call the **Teacher's Copy Captions** first. **Play the game many times until the children are successful.**
When the students are ready, call the **Enrichment Captions**. These captions contain new vocabulary but are designed to teach the children to use context clues to find the correct picture.

CHAPTER 1

Objectives - To teach: listening to a dialogue - speaking in a role-play - vocabulary – sentence structure – naming "Aa" – listening to and identifying the short ă sound at the beginning of a word. Identifying auditory differences.

We strongly suggest that you teach the Alphabet Song as music is located in a different part of the brain. Learning the words to a song is easier than learning a sentence.
We hope that our Alphabet Song available at the address shown below will help you.

The Alphabet song: https://youtu.be/Xdlh-eZyGJk

The Teacher's Guide Picture Bingo 1 can be used when the children have finished Chapter 4.
Test 1: This test can be given directly after Chapter 4 or after the students have played Picture Bingo 1.

Read the conversation to the class.

Say: "My name is _____."   **Ask each child for a small class: For a large class, ask some children.**

Ask: "What is your name?" *(My name is _____.)*

Review dialogue several times.   **Ask:** Do Elizabeth and George have fun? *(Yes, they do.)*   **Say:** Let's go with them.

Have them **role-play** in the large group and small groups.
When asking questions to individuals in the whole group, choose the children randomly so they don't know who you will ask next. This keeps them attending.   **Important:** Always review the story before starting a new Lesson.

Children learn by listening and repeating. They will understand the new vocabulary by looking at the pictures and using the context of the dialogue. The Workbook and Teacher's Guide provide a great deal of repetition.

Student Reader

CHAPTER 1 CONTINUED

Explain that panda bears live among the bamboo and eats the leaves. Read the dialogue orally several times.

Explain: This letter's name is "Aa". Big A and small a say the same thing.

Ask: What is the teacher's name? (*His name is Panda Bear.*)

Ask: What is the letter's name? (*Its name is "Aa"*)

Say: "alligator" stressing the first sound. **Explain: Aa** is its name but it says ă, the first sound in apple.

Say: "apple" stressing the first sound. **Have the children say** "apple" and "alligator" several times.

WORKBOOK PAGE 2

Student Reader

CHAPTER 1 CONTINUED

Alligators eat apples.

Do you eat apples?

Yes, we eat apples!

I want to see the baboons.

Read the dialogue orally and have the students read it with you several times, having the children point to the words and pictures as they read.
Have the children say the words as they point to: George, Elizabeth, Panda Bear, alligator, apple, children.
Ask: Do you eat apples? (Yes, we eat apples.) **(Try to have a "Yes" answer.)**   **WORKBOOK PAGES 3-4**

Student Reader

CHAPTER 2

baboons

Read what Panda Bear is saying several times.

Have the children point to **B** and say "**capital B**". Then point to **b** and say "**small b**"

Have the children point to the baboons and repeat the name several times.

Point to the picture and count the baboons: **1, 2. Have the whole class** count with you: **1, 2.**

Ask: How many baboons? **Say:** *There are two baboons.*

Ask again: Have them answer in unison. *(There are two baboons.)*

NOTE: The storybook characters will go to see dangerous animals on a screen.
They'll interact with friendly animals.

Information: Baboons live on savannahs and in forests in Africa. They require access to water.
They can climb trees and use them to sleep. They are omnivores and hunters. They eat roots, bark, seeds, rodents, birds and young larger animals,
They travel in groups communicating with grunts, screams barks and body language.   **WORKBOOK PAGE 5**

Student Reader

CHAPTER 2 CONTINUED

The baby baboon has a ball.

The mother has a banana.

We're getting a cat!

Important: Before you introduce a new lesson **review the story** so far as appropriate for your class.

Ask: What animal do you see? (I/We see baboons.)

Ask: How many baboons do you see? (I/We see two baboons.)

Ask: What is this letter's name? (Its name is Bb.) **Ask:** What is the first letter in baboon? (Bb is the first letter.)

Ask: What does the baby baboon have? (It has a ball.) **Ask:** What does the mother have? (She has a banana.)

Ask: Do you have a ball? (Yes, I have a ball.) (No, I don't have a ball.)

Ask: Do you have a banana? (Yes, I have a banana.) (No, I don't have a banana.)

NOTE: The small figures at the end of each chapter tell what will happen next. Discuss as appropriate.

WORKBOOK PAGE 6
TEACHER'S GUIDE: THE STUDENTS WILL BE READY FOR THE PICTURE BINGO GAMES AFTER CHAPTER 4.

Student Reader

CHAPTER 3

Say: Point to the cat. **Ask:** What is the cat's name? (*Its name is Cassie.*) **Ask:** Is the cat friendly? (*Yes, it's friendly.*)
Say: Point to the cat. **Ask:** Where is the cat. (*The cat is in the tree.*) **Ask:** Can the cat climb? (*Yes, it can.*)
WORKBOOK PAGE 7

Student Reader

CHAPTER 3 CONTINUED

Teach: The children always read the role-plays from left to right. This is important as some languages are different.

Point to Cc. **Ask:** What is this letter's name? *(Its name is "Cc".)*

Ask: What is the first letter in cat? *(The first letter is C.)* **Ask:** What is the first letter in climb? *(The first letter is C.)*

Ask: Can cats climb? *(Yes, they can.)* **Ask some children:** Can you climb? *(Yes, I can. No, I can't.)*

Go to: the picture on the bottom right. **Ask:** What help do you think Cassie needs?

Ask: Who will need help? *(Cassie will need help.)*

WORKBOOK PAGE 8   GUIDE: PLAY PICTURE BINGO AFTER CHAPTER 4.

Student Reader

CHAPTER 3 CONTINUED

Role-play: **Ask:** Who gets Cassie down? *(Diego gets Cassie down.)* **Ask:** What does Cassie say? *(She says meow.)*
GUIDE: BINGO INSTRUCTIONS: PAGE 2 FOR PICTURE BINGO 1

Student Reader

CHAPTER 4

Read the dialogue to the children and point to Dd.   **Say** – listen to the first sound: **dinosaur, dog, dangerous**.
Have the children repeat dinosaur, dog, dangerous - stressing the first sound and pointing to the words on their books.

Ask: Do dinosaurs live here? (*No, they don't live here.*)   **Role-play** the dialogue many times.

Ask: Would you love your dog? (*Yes, I would!*) Review story. **Ask**: Where are George and Elizabeth going to go?
(*They are going to go to the park.*)

WORKBOOK PAGE 9   **GUIDE: PICTURE BINGO 1 PAGES 3-29**

Student Reader

CHAPTER 5

Explain: Elizabeth and George are at an animal park. Elizabeth is thinking about elephants. **Point** to the elf on the gate.
Ask: Do you think the elf is a magician? (*Yes or No*)   **Ask:** What is Elizabeth thinking? (She thinks about elephants.)
Role-play.   **DO WORKBOOK BEFORE TEST 1: PAGES 10 – 11**
GUIDE: TEST FOR CHAPTERS 1-4: PAGES 30-31

Student Reader

CHAPTER 5 CONTINUED

This is **Ee**

This is an elephant.

I don't think that elf is a magician!

I think he's a magician!

Let's go to the pond.

Have the children point to Ee and say its name.

Explain: Its name is Ee but it says the first sound in "**elf**" and "**elephant**"

Read the dialogue and have the children role-play, taking turns with different storybook characters.

Note: George thinks that the elf is a magician so he emphasis the "**I**" as he speaks.

Ask: Where are George and Elizabeth going to go? (*They're going to go to the pond.*)

WORKBOOK PAGE 12
GUIDE: CONTINUE WITH CHAPTERS 1-4 PICTURE BINGO1 AS APPROPRIATE.

Student Reader

CHAPTER 6

Explain that the children have gone into the park and found a pond. George says it's a **cool** pond. **Read and role-play.**

Ask: Does he like the park? (*Yes, he does!*) **Ask:** What has he caught? (*He's caught a fish.*)

Ask: What has Elizabeth caught? (*She's caught a frog.*) **Ask:** Would you want to catch a frog? (*Yes, I would. No, I wouldn't.*)

Ask: Would you want to catch a fish? (*Yes, I would. No, I wouldn't.*)

WORKBOOK PAGE 13   GUIDE PICTURE BINGO AS APPROPRIATE

Student Reader

CHAPTER 6 CONTINUED

This is **Ff**

What is this?

It's a fish.

What are these?

They are frogs.

Let's go to see the geese.

Introduce Ff. **Point** to the fish, then the frogs. Have the children repeat "**fish**" and "**frogs**".

Say: **Ff** is the first letter in fish and frogs.   **Explain:** Panda Bear is asking questions, George and Elizabeth answer.

Role-play many times.   **Ask:** Do you like fish? (*Yes, I do. / No, I don't.*)

Ask: Would you want to have a frog? (*Yes, I would. / No, I wouldn't.*)   **Ask:** What they will do next.

WORKBOOK: PAGES 14   **GUIDE: PICTURE BINGO 1 AS APPROPRIATE**

Student Reader

CHAPTER 7

Read the dialogue orally. Explain that the mother goose is keeping the baby warm under her wing. **Explain:** "guarding"
Role-play several times. **Ask:** How does the mother keep the baby warm? (*She keeps it under her wing.*)
Ask: What is the father doing? (*He's guarding the mother and baby.*) **WORKBOOK PAGE 15, PICTURE BINGO 1**

Student Reader

CHAPTER 7 CONTINUED

Explain what is happening in the picture. The mother goose is keeping her babies warm. The goat is looking at the mother. The father is attacking the goat. He is protecting the mother and baby..

Introduce: "attacking" and "protecting". **Role-play.** **Ask:** Is the goat dangerous? (No, it isn't dangerous.)

Ask: Will the goat will run? (Yes, I think it will run.) **Ask:** Would you run? (Yes, I'd run!) (No, I wouldn't run.)

GUIDE PICTURE BINGO 1 AS APPROPRIATE

Student Reader

CHAPTER 7 CONTINUED

Introduce Gg. Explain: The father goose is called a gander, the mother is a goose, and the babies are goslings. Have the children point to the words and pictures and say the names stressing the first sound **g**. Repeat for goat.

Role-play the dialogue.   **Ask:** What does George want to do? *(He wants to watch the goslings.)*

Ask: What does Elizabeth want to do? *(She wants to talk to the goat.)* **Ask:** What would you want to do? *(I'd want to...)*

WORKBOOK PAGE 16   GUIDE: CONTINUE WITH PICTURE BINGO 1

Student Reader

CHAPTER 8

Read the dialogue orally. Explain that cowboys wear hats when they look after animals.

Explain: George is wearing his Uncle Brian's hat.

Have the children point to the horse / hat. Say "horse" "hat" stressing the Hh.

Print "horse" "hat" on the board underlining the h in each word. Role-play the dialogue several times.

Ask: What do the children want to do? (They want to ride a horse.)

Ask: What is George wearing? (He's wearing his Uncle Brian's hat.)

Ask: Would you want to ride a horse? (Yes, I would.) (No, I wouldn't.)

Ask: Does Elizabeth want to ride? (Yes, she does.)

WORKBOOK PAGE 17   GUIDE: CONTINUE WITH PICTURE BINGO 1

CHAPTER 8 CONTINUED

Explain: The horses are in a big field in the park. They have been eating the hay that is around their feet. The children are allowed to sit on the horse's backs. George was wearing his uncle's hat but it fell off because it's too big.

Read the dialogue with the children several times. **Role-play** changing roles.

Say: Point to the hay. **Ask:** What do horses eat? (Horses eat hay.) **Ask:** Do we eat hay? (No, we don't.)

Ask: Where is the hat? (It's in the hay.) **Ask:** What is Elizabeth doing? (She's getting on the horse.)

Ask: What color is the hay? (It's brown.) **Ask:** Would you want to sit on a horse? (Yes, I would.) (No, I wouldn't!)

WORKBOOK: PAGE 18

Student Reader

CHAPTER 8 CONTINUED

This is **Hh**

Say: horse.
Say: horses
Say: hat
Say: hay

I got my Uncle Brian's hat from the hay!

That was fun!

Let's see the iguanas.

Explain: The children have returned to the park the next day to visit the horses.

Introduce Hh. As the children follow Panda Bear's directions, they are to point to the object or objects stressing the first sound in each word as they speak

Role-play.   **Ask:** How many horses are there? *(There are 2 horses.)* **Ask:** How many hats do you see? *(I see 1 hat.)*

Ask: Do you like horses? *(Yes, I like horses.)* *(No, I don't like horses.)*

Ask: Would you like ride the horses? *(Yes, I would!)* *(No, I wouldn't!)* **Ask:** What will they see next? *(They'll see iguanas)*

WORKBOOK PAGES 19-20   **GUIDE TEST 2: PAGE 59-60**
GUIDE PICTURE BINGO 2: PAGE 32

Student Reader

CHAPTER 9

This is **I i**

Iguanas live in the warm jungle.

They're good climbers!

I wish I could climb like that.

Explain: The children are visiting the iguanas in the park. Read the dialogue several times.
Have the children role-play the dialogue speaking together and role-play in groups or individually.
Say: Put your finger on an orange iguana. **Say:** Put your finger on a green iguana.
Ask: Are the iguanas good climbers?? *(Yes, they are.)*
Ask: What does Elizabeth wish she could do? *(She wishes she could climb like the iguanas.)*
Ask: Can you climb like an iguana? *(Yes, I can.) (No, I can't.)*

WORKBOOK PAGE 21   GUIDE PICTURE BINGO 2: PAGES 32-58

Student Reader

CHAPTER 9 CONTINUED

"Iguanas are friendly."

"They eat green leaves."

"They would make a friendly pet!"

"I like my cat, Cassie."

"I want to see the jackals."

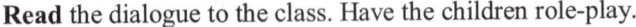

Read the dialogue to the class. Have the children role-play.

Ask: Are the iguanas friendly? (*Yes, they are.*)   **Ask:** Are you friendly? (*Yes, we are.*) or (*Yes, I am.*)

Ask: What are the iguanas doing? (*They are eating leaves.*) **Ask:** Do we eat leaves? (*Yes, we do.*)

Ask: What colors are the iguanas in the picture? (*They are orange and green*)

Ask: Would you want a pet iguana? (*Yes, I would.*) (*No, I wouldn't*)

WORKBOOK: PAGE 22   GUIDE: CONTINUE WITH PICTURE BINGO 2

CHAPTER 10

Read what Panda Bear is saying and the dialogue, having the children read it in unison with you several times.
Explain: Jackals are wild animals, they aren't friendly.

Ask: Are jackals friendly? (No, they aren't friendly.)   **Ask:** Are most dogs friendly? (Yes, most dogs are friendly.)

Ask: Do you think they look like dogs? (Yes, I think they look like dogs.) (No, I don't think they look like dogs.)

Ask: Where do the jackals live? (They live near the trees.)   **Ask:** What do jackals eat? (They eat dead animals and fish.)

Note: Some of these questions are difficult. Adapt them for your class.

WORKBOOK: PAGE 23   GUIDE: CONTINUE WITH PICTURE BINGO 2

Student Reader

CHAPTER 10 CONTINUED

Explain: Jaguars hunt at night in the jungle and in the grass beside the trees. They are very dangerous animals that kill other animals to eat their meat. They are predators. Discuss this as appropriate for your class.

Ask: Are jaguars friendly? (*No, they aren't friendly.*)   **Ask:** Can they climb trees? (*Yes, they can climb trees.*)

Ask: Are jaguars dangerous? (*Yes, they are.*)

Ask: Would you want to meet a jaguar? (*No, I wouldn't want to meet a jaguar.*)

Ask: What do jaguars eat? (*They eat meat.*)   **Ask:** Do we eat meat? (*Yes, we eat meat.*) (*No, we don't eat meat.*)

Ask: What do George and Elizabeth want to do? (*They want to pet the baby animals.*)

WORKBOOK: PAGE 24
OR INTRODUCE BINGO 4 PAGE 89-115

GUIDE: REVIEW PICTURE BINGO PAGE 62
GUIDE: TEST 3 PAGE 87-88

Student Reader

CHAPTER 11

Explain that baby goats are called kids. If appropriate tell the class that children are called kids, too.
Read the dialogue orally and have the children role-play it several times.

Ask: What did Elizabeth want to do? (*She wanted to catch the kids.*) **Ask:** Did she catch a kid? (*Yes, she did.*)

Ask: Are the kids high jumpers? (*Yes, they are.*) **Ask:** What is George's kid doing? (*It's jumping.*)

Ask: Are you high jumpers? (*Yes, we are.*) or (*Yes, I am.*)

WORKBOOK: PAGE 25 GUIDE BINGO 4 PAGE 89-115

Student Reader

CHAPTER 11 CONTINUED

"These lambs have soft warm wool."

"They want to climb on their mother. I want to swing on this branch."

"Will you run with me?"

"Let's see the lions!"

Explain: The mother is a sheep. The babies are lambs. They have soft warm wool.

Have the children point to the mother sheep / lambs.

Ask: How many lambs are standing on the mother sheep? (*One lamb is standing on its mother.*)

Have the children point to George.

Ask: What is George doing? (*He's swinging on a branch.*)

Role-play the dialogue several times having the groups change roles.

Ask: Do you have a warm wool coat? (*Yes, I have a warm wool coat.*) (*No, I don't have a warm wool coat.*)

Ask: Would you like to swing on a branch? (*Yes, I'd like to swing on a branch.*) (*No, I wouldn't like to swing on a branch.*)

GUIDE: PICTURE BINGO 4 PAGE 89-115

Student Reader

CHAPTER 12

This is **L l**

Speech bubbles:
- What were you doing?
- I was looking at the mother sheep.
- Those lions are dangerous!
- They're wild animals.

Explain: Lions live in a hot country. The lion cubs are with their father. He is cleaning the cub's ear.

Read the role-play to the children several times. **Directions:** Have the children role-play the dialogue.

Ask: What did Elizabeth ask George? *(She asked, "Where were you doing?")*

Ask: What was George doing? *(He was looking at the mother sheep.)*

Ask: Are the lions dangerous? *Yes, they are dangerous.)* **Ask:** Are lions wild animals? *(Yes, they are.)*

DO WORKBOOK BEFORE TEST: PAGES 28-31   GUIDE: FINAL TEST PAGES 116-121

Student Reader

ESL ANIMALS 1

The Alphabet A to L

Student Workbook

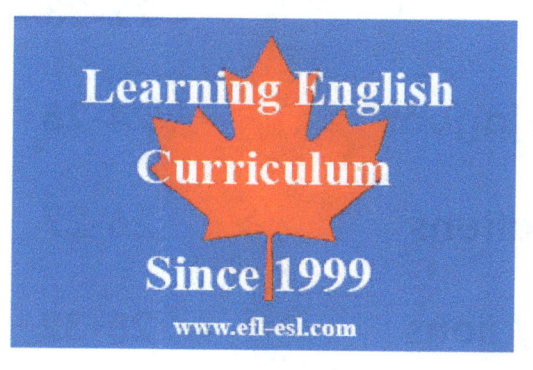

Daisy A. Stocker M.Ed.
George A. Stocker D.D.S.

ESL ANIMALS 1

WORKBOOK

CONTENTS

			PAGES
Introduction			1
Chapter 1	Aa	alligator	2-4
Chapter 2	Bb	baboons	5-6
Chapter 3	Cc	cat	7-8
Chapter 4	Dd	dinosaur	9-11
Chapter 5	Ee	elephant	12-13
Chapter 6	Ff	fish / frog	14-15
Chapter 7	Gg	goat / goose	16-17
Chapter 8	Hh	horse / review	18-21
Chapter 9	Ii	iguana	22-23
Chapter 10	Jj	jackal/jaguar	24-25
Chapter 11	Kk	kids / kittens	26-27
Chapter 12	Ll	lambs / lions	28-32

ESL ANIMALS 1
A to L

WORKBOOK
CHAPTERS 1 to 12

The Student Reader is presented in a graphics novel format stressing listening, speaking, understanding, writing and phonics. It introduces the alphabet letters from A to L and associates them with animals, birds and food. Numbers from 1 to 12 are included. It is designed for children aged 6 to 8 years who have matured past the need for reading readiness and fine motor control practice. The children will see wild animals on the screen.

The **Student Reader** can be used by many different classes as the children don't write in it. Teacher instructions are given in smaller print at the bottom of each page. The suggestions provide oral practice and enhance student understanding. Page number references to the Workbook and Guide are at the bottom of each page.

This Reader introduces the alphabet from A to L with pictures and simple dialogue for role-plays. The children are introduced to their teacher, a panda bear. He explains the names and sounds of the letters, using key words and pictures. The two storybook characters, George and Elizabeth, introduce themselves. They speak to the children in your class saying, "We have fun." They then invite everyone in the class to join their adventures. At the end of each chapter George and Elizabeth introduce the next lesson by talking about what they are going to do next.

The **Workbook** teaches printing on lines using key word examples. It provides the children with many opportunities to participate with the storybook characters. Teacher suggestions are provided in small print on each page. These guide the teacher in presenting the lessons in the best way.

Panda Bear, the teacher, names the letter and models what they say. The children have practice printing the letters and key words between the lines. Understanding of the key words is reinforced with colorful pictures. The numbers are introduced with the oral counting of a series of pictures.

The **Teacher's Guide** includes **Tests** to be given after lesson Chapters 4, 10 1nd 12. The **Picture Bingo** games review and reinforce the children's understanding of the materials taught. These are very important as they motivate the children to attend and understand.

Call the **Teacher's Captions** first. **Play the game many times until the children are successful.** When the students are ready, call the **Enrichment Captions**. These captions contain new vocabulary but are designed to teach the children to use context clues to find the correct picture.

Student Workbook

CHAPTER 1

This is **Aa**

apple

a

apple

alligator

A

Alligator

Read what Panda Bear says.
Point to the alligator. **Say:** alligator
Say: "apple" Have the children say it stressing the first sound.
Ask: Is the first sound ă? (*Yes it is.*)

Have the whole class say "apple, alligator" in unison. Speaking together will help everyone to participate.

Teach: You say many things but Aa says the first sound in apple.

Ask: Do you have a name? **Point** to "Aa". **Ask:** What is its name? (*Its name is Aa*) (as in the alphabet.)

As you introduce the printing, Refer to "A" as "**capital A**". Refer to "a" as "**small a**",

Note: Point out the difference in size, tall letters and those that extend below the line.

Student Workbook

2

CHAPTER 1 CONTINUED

Have the children point as you say: apple, alligator, rabbit.

Say: Circle the ones that start with ă

Have the children point as you say: car, apple, alligator,

Say: Circle the ones that start with ă.

Have the children point as you say:: rabbit, car, alligator.

Say: Circle the one that starts with ă.

Say: Here is **1** big apple.

Have them point to the top of the big apple and the number **1**.

They are to color the **1**'s red starting at the top.

Have them point to the small apples.

Have them point to the capital **A**'s.

Next have them point to the small **a**'s

They are to draw **blue** circles around the capital **A**'s.

Draw **green** circles around the small **a**'s.

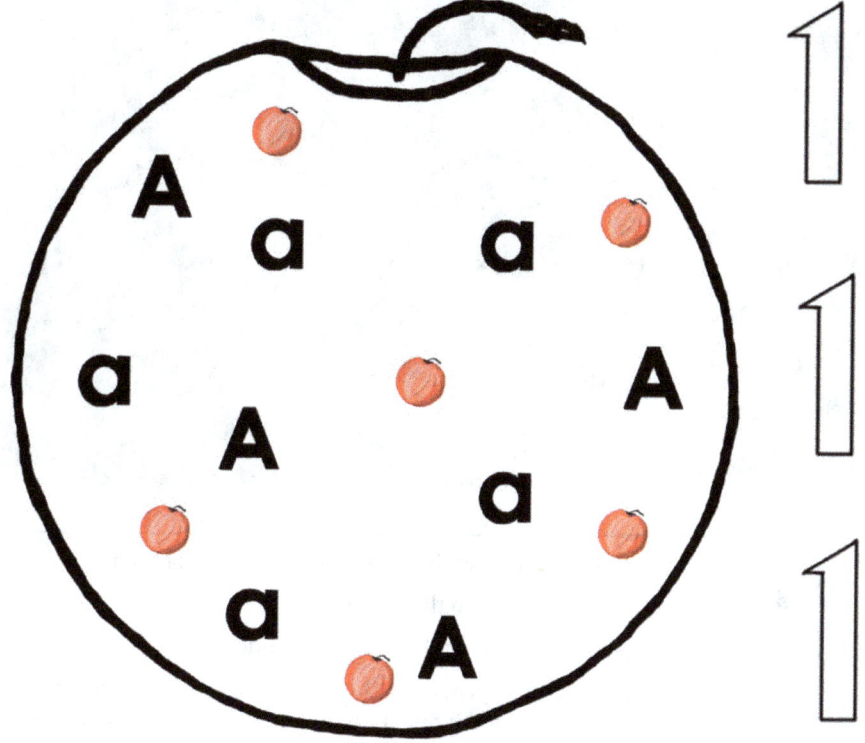

| **Point** to **1:** | **Say:** There is one big apple. | Have the children point to the top of the big apple and say "1". |

Student Workbook

CHAPTER 1 CONTINUED

Will the alligator eat the rabbit?

Help the rabbit to hide!

Hide here.

Explain: The rabbit is hiding in the grass. The alligator is hungry!

Say: Point to the rabbit. Point to the alligator.

Say: Color the path to show the rabbit where to hide

The children are to use their pencils to show the path that leads to the "Hide here" sign".
If some children suggest that the rabbit could jump the pond or jump over the grass where the path ends, accept their suggestions. **Always encourage imagination!** However, tell them that they must express their idea by drawing it on the picture.

Student Workbook

CHAPTER 2

 baboon

b

baboon

B

Ball

The children point to Bb at the top of the page.:   **Say:** Its name is Bb.   **Ask:** What is its name? (Its name is Bb.)

Point to and read what Panda Bear says orally, the children are to repeat it several times.

Say: The first sound in "baboon" is "Bb". This is **small b**. This is **capital B**.

Point to the baboon.   **Say: "baboon"** stressing the first sound.

Point to the ball.   **Say: "ball"** Name the colors, red and green.

Note: Point out how the letters sit on the line. Have the children print the letter and the words on the lines.

Student Workbook

CHAPTER 2 CONTINUED

George is a **boy**.

He has a big **ball**.

Have the children point as you say: ball, apple, baboon.

Say: Circle the ones that start with **Bb**.

Have the children point as you say: alligator, baboon, ball.

Say: Circle the ones that start with **Bb**.

Have the children point as you say: boy, rabbit, baboon.

Say: Circle the ones that start with **Bb**.

Point to the dogs as you count: "one, two".

Say: Everyone point and count – one, two.

Note: Check that the children coordinate their hand movement, pointing to each number as they count. Some children will find this difficult.

Have the children use their crayons to trace the numbers, starting at the top.

Here are 2 dogs.

2 2 2
2 2 2

Student Workbook

6

CHAPTER 3

c

cat

C

Cat

The children point to the cat and the capital **C**.	**Say:** This is capital **C**. Its name is **C**.
Ask: What is its name? *(Its name is C.)*	**Ask:** What does it say? *(It says the first sound in cat.)*

Note: Try to avoid separating the sound of the letter as it changes with different consonant blends. It is better to stress the sound as you say the word.

Introduce "small c" in the same way. Review its name: **Small c**

Have the children print the letters and words on the lines.

Student Workbook

CHAPTER 3 CONTINUED

Hi, I'm a clown.

The first letter in **clown** is **c**.

Have the children point as you say: Say: cat, clown, duck. Circle the ones that start with **Cc**.	
Have the children point as you say: car, boat, clown. **Say:** Circle the ones that start with **Cc**.	
Have the children point as you say: clown, ball, crayons. **Say:** Circle the ones that start with **Cc**.	

Here are 3 crayons.

You count them, 1, 2, 3.

Follow the directions in the boxes.
Read what the clown is saying and have the children repeat it several times.

Have the children point to each crayon as they count. **Ask:** How many crayons does the clown have? (*He has three.*)

Ask: What color are the crayons? (*They are yellow, blue and red.*)

Student Workbook

8

CHAPTER 4

This **Dd**

I'm a dangerous dinosaur!

d

dinosaur

D

Dinosaur

Have the children point to the letter Dd.	**Read** what Panda Bear is saying. Have them repeat it after you.
Read what the dinosaur is saying and have the students repeat it in unison.	
Ask: Is this dinosaur dangerous? (Yes, it is!)	**Say:** Print the letters and words on the lines.

Student Workbook

CHAPTER 4 CONTINUED

I love my doll. Her name is Dorothy.

Have the children point as you say: Say: duck, clown, dinosaur.

Circle the ones that start with Dd.

Have the children point as you say: Say: cat, dog, doll.

Circle the ones that start with Dd.

Have the children point as you say: Say: doll, cat, duck.

Circle the ones that start with Dd.

Count the dogs, 1 2 3 4.

Read the dialogues orally and have the children repeat. Introduce the page in the same way as Page 8.
Printing "4". The students start at the top, draw down on the diagonal and across, then lift their crayons and draw down.

Student Workbook

CHAPTER 4 CONTINUED

Have the children point to the pictures in the big duck as you say their names, moving from top to bottom and left to right.: **clown, doll, ball, dinosaur, ant, duck, alligator.**

They are to circle the ones with the first sound of **Dd**.

Have the children say the names of the four letters in unison.

Next have them name the pictures from left to right stressing the first sound: **doll, clown, apple, ball.**

They are to draw a line from each letter to the picture with that sound.

Student Workbook

11

CHAPTER 5

e

elf

E

Elephant

Have the children read what Panda Bear is saying. "This is Ee." **Have them point** to the elf and the elephant.

Explain: Its name is Ee but it says the first sound in "elephant - elf"
Have the children point to the elf and say its name several times stressing the first sound. Repeat for "elephant".

Point to the elf's hat.   **Ask:** What color is the elf's hat? *(It's green..)*

Ask: What color are the elf's pants? *(They're blue.)*

Ask: What color is the elf's shirt? *(It's yellow)*

Student Workbook

CHAPTER 5 CONTINUED

Color the elf's hat red.

Color his pants green.

Color his shirt. yellow.

Count the elephants. 1 2 3 4 5.

5 5 5 5 5

___ ___ ___ ___ ___

Introduce what Panda Bear is saying. Have the children point to the elf's hat, pants and shirt. Review colors.

Introduce "5" The children are to print the 5's.

Say: How many elephants? Let's count them. Children point as they count, then print the numbers on the lines.

Student Workbook

CHAPTER 6

This is **F f**

f

frog

fish

F

Fish

Have the children point to and read what Panda Bear is saying. Have the class read the words.

Explain: Its name is **Ff,** but it says the first sound in "**frog – fish**".
Have the children point to the frog and say its name several times stressing the first sound. Repeat for "fish".

Ask: Would you like to catch a frog? *(Yes, I would.) (No, I wouldn't.)*

Ask: Would you like to catch a fish? *(Yes, I would.) (No, I wouldn't.)*

The children are to print the letters and the words on the lines.

CHAPTER 6 CONTINUED

You caught a fish!

Draw your fish!

Draw your hair.

Draw your shirt blue.

Draw your shoes black.

Draw your pants or skirt green.

This is 6

1 2 3 4 5 6

Read what the teacher is saying. **Teach** "hair, shirt, shoes, pants, skirt" by having the children point to their own clothes. Have the children point to the figure and point to where they will draw the clothes. Girls draw skirts or pants.

Read what the teacher says and have the children count to 6. They are to print the 6's in the box.

Say: Point to your hair, shirt, pants, skirt, shoes. Review as needed.

Student Workbook

CHAPTER 7

goat

g

goat

goose

G

Goose

> Have the children point to and read what Panda Bear is saying.
>
> **Explain:** Its name is **Gg** but it says the first sound in "goat, goose"
> Have the children point to the goat and say its name several times stressing the first sound. Repeat for "goose".
>
> **Ask:** Would you like to have a goat? (*Yes, I would.*) (*No, I wouldn't.*)
>
> **Ask:** Does the mother goose have a gosling? (*Yes, she does.*) (*No, she doesn't.*)
>
> Have the students print the letters and words on the lines.

Student Workbook

CHAPTER 7 CONTINUED

Gander

Say 7.
Count the goslings:
Print the 7's.
Print
1 2 3
4 5 6 7
under the goslings.

Mother Goose and Gosling

Goat

___ ___ ___

___ ___ ___ ___

> Have the children point to the pictures and read their names.
> Continue with Panda Bear's directions for "7".
> **Ask:** How many mother geese are on this page? (There is 1 mother goose.)
> **Ask:** How many ganders are on this page? (There is 1 gander.)
> **Ask:** How many goats are there? (There is 1 goat.)

Student Workbook

CHAPTER 8

This is **Hh**

horse

h

horse

hay

H

Hat

Have the children point to and read what Panda Bear is saying.

Explain: Its name is **Hh** but it says the first sound in **horse, hat**.

Ask: Would you like to have a horse? (*Yes, I would.*) (*No, I wouldn't.*)   **Ask:** Do horses eat hay? (*Yes, they do.*)

Ask: Do you eat hay? (*No, I don't!*)   **Ask**: Do you have a hat? (*Yes, I do.*) (*No, I don't.*)

Ask: What color is your hat? (*My hat is _____.*)   The students are to print the letters and words on the line.

Student Workbook

CHAPTER 8 CONTINUED

George needs help! Draw George getting out of the hay.

Help!

I'll help!

This is **8**
Count the 8's.
Print:
1,2,3,4,5,6,7,8

8 8 8 8
8 8 8 8

Introduce: George has jumped into the hay. **Ask?** Does George need help? (*Yes, he does.*)
Instructions: Have them print the numbers under the hats **Ask:** Would you help George? (*Yes, I would.*) (*No, I wouldn't.*)

Student Workbook

CHAPTER 8 CONTINUED

Count the number you see in each picture.

Draw a line from the number to the picture.

4

5

2

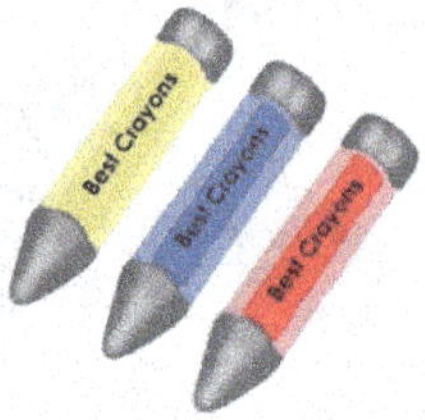

6

7

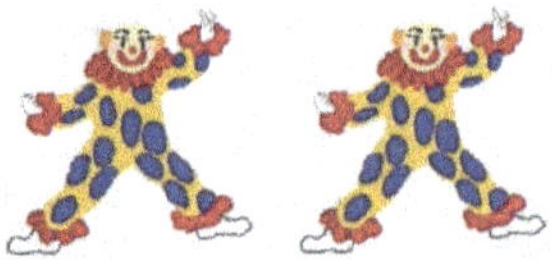

3

1

8

Introduce: Panda Bear's instructions.   **Say:** Let's name the pictures.
goslings, frogs, dolls, crayons, clowns, kittens, apple, hats
Count the number of figures in each box with the children as needed.
They are to draw a line from each number to the appropriate picture.

Student Workbook

20

CHAPTER 8 CONTINUED

Draw a line from the picture to the word that tells its name.

 fish

clown

apple

 boat

gander

 doll

hat

 elf

Note: This review is the first independent reading activity. Pay special attention to how well the children do as this will alert you as to how much emphasis you put on reading in the coming lessons.

Directions: Have the children point to each picture and say its name. Read the words aloud to them if appropriate.

From left to right they are: **clown, fish, doll, boat, apple, elf, gander, hat**

Student Workbook

CHAPTER 9

i

iguana

I

Iguana

The students point to and read what Panda Bear is saying. **Ask:** Would you like to have an iguana for a pet? Have the children print the letters and words on the lines. **Ask:** How many orange iguanas do you see? (I (*We*) see 1 orange iguana.) **Ask:** How many green iguanas do you see? (I (*We*) see 1 green iguana.) **Note:** Sometimes the capital **I** and small **l** (**L**) are shown as the same. This children's font shows them that way. Explain this if the students ask. They will adapt using the context of the sentence.	**Explain:** Its name is **Ii** but it says the first sound in iguana. (*Yes, I'd like to have an iguana for a pet.*) (*No, I wouldn't like to have an iguana for a pet.*)

Student Workbook

CHAPTER 9 CONTINUED

This is 9

Count all the iguanas. 1 2 3 4 5 6 7 8 9

Print a number on each iguana.

Have the children read Panda Bear's instructions with you.

Note: They are to point to the iguanas and say the numbers as they count.

1 has been printed on the first iguana at the top left.

Ask: What are the iguanas doing? (*They are eating.*)   **Ask:** What do they eat? (*They eat leaves.*)

Student Workbook

CHAPTER 10

j

jackal

J

Jaguar

Have the children read what Panda Bear says, then read the names of the animals.

The children point to the letter **Jj** and say its name. **Explain:** Its name is **Jj** but it says the first sound in jackal / jaguar

Ask: Are jackals friendly? *(No, they aren't friendly.)*   **Ask:** Are jaguars friendly? *(No, they aren't friendly.)*

Ask: Do jackals eat meat? (Yes, they do.)   **Ask:** Do jaguars eat meat? (Yes, they do.)

Have the students print the letters and words on the lines.

Student Workbook

CHAPTER 10 CONTINUED

Jaguars live in the hot jungle.

They hunt other animals for food.

Let's count the baby jaguars.
1 2 3 4 5 6 7 8 9 10

____ ____ ____ ____ ____   ____ ____ ____ ____ ____

Say: Put your finger on the **jungle** / **jaguar**. **Have the children say**: jungle, jaguar.
Ask: What is the first letter in jaguar? (*The first letter in jaguar is Jj.*) **Repeat** the question for "jungle".
Read the first two lines of what Panda Bear is saying and have the children read it with you several times.
Ask: Where do the jaguars live? (*They live in the hot jungle.*)   **Ask:** Is the jungle hot? (*Yes, it is.*)
Ask: What do they hunt? (*They hunt other animals.*)   **Ask:** Why do they hunt other animals? (*They want food.*)
Ask: Do you eat food? (*Yes, we /Yes, I do.*) **Instructions:** Have the children point to the baby jaguars and count them.
Ask: How many baby jaguars are there? (*There are 10 baby jaguars.*)   They are to print the numbers 1 to 10.

Student Workbook

CHAPTER 11

This is **Kk**

This baby goat is called a kid.
That baby cat is called a kitten.

k

kid

K

Kitten

Have the children read what Panda Bear says several times.

Have them point to **Kk** and say its name.   **Explain:** Its name is **Kk** but it says the first sounds in kid and kitten.

Have the children say: kid, kitten.   **Ask:** What is a baby goat called? *(It's called a kid.)*

Ask: What is a baby cat called? *(It'd called a kitten.)*   **Ask:** Are kids friendly? *(Yes, they are.)*

Ask: Are kittens friendly? *(Yes, they are.)*   Have the class print the letters and words.

Student Workbook

CHAPTER 11 CONTINUED

Say: Put your fingers on the **kittens / kids** and have the children say: **kittens / kids** as they point. **Role-play.** **The students are to print** the numbers 1 to 11 under the kittens.

Ask: What do the kittens like to do? (*They like to play and sleep.*)

Ask: What do the kids like to do? (*They like to run and jump.*)

Ask: How many animals are with Elizabeth and George? (*There are four animals... or... with Elizabeth and George.*

Student Workbook

CHAPTER 12

This is **L l**

lambs

l

lambs

lions

L

Lion

Have the children read what Panda Bear says, then have them read the names of the animals.

Have them point to **Ll** and say its name.   **Explain:** Its name is **Ll** but it says the first sounds in lamb and lion.

Have the children say: **lamb, lion**.   **Ask:** Are lambs friendly? *(Yes, they are.)*

Ask: Are lions friendly? *(No, they aren't friendly.)*

Have the class print the letters and words.

Student Workbook

CHAPTER 12 CONTINUED

Have the children point to the animals and name them from left to right.
horse, bird, iguana, dog, frogs, cat, kitten, goose, goslings

Say: Point to the one that starts with **Bb**. Repeat: using the first letter of each word.

You might want to divide them into several groups. **Role-play** the conversation.

Ask: What animal would you like to have? List the children's choices on the board.

Put a check mark after the name of the duplicates. Point out the most popular and discuss why.

Student Workbook

WORKBOOK REVIEW 1

Have the children point to the pictures from left to right and name them:
bird, cat. iguana, horse, dog, elephant, fish, gander, jaguar, lambs

They are to draw a line from each picture to the letter that tells its first sound.

Give help if some children don't remember the name. This is a sound/symbol review exercise.

Student Workbook

WORKBOOK REVIEW 2

7
5
3
4
11
12
8
2
9
10
6

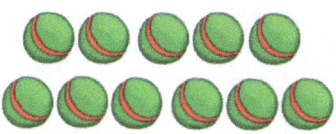

Have the children point to the pictures and name them:
crayons, kittens, lambs, elephants, balls, goslings, hats, cars, clowns, boats, frogs

They are to draw a line from each number to the picture that shows that many.

NOTE NEW VOCABULARY: crayons, cars, clowns.

Student Workbook

WORKBOOK REVIEW 3

Introduction: The children are to point to the pictures as you say the names from left to right.
dinosaur, boat, apple, jackal, gander, kitten, frog, lions

Directions: The children are to draw a line from each object to the first letter (sound) in its name.

Note: Give help if some children don't remember the creature's name. This exercise is sound/ symbol review.

Student Workbook

ESL ANIMALS 1

The Alphabet A to L

Teacher Guide

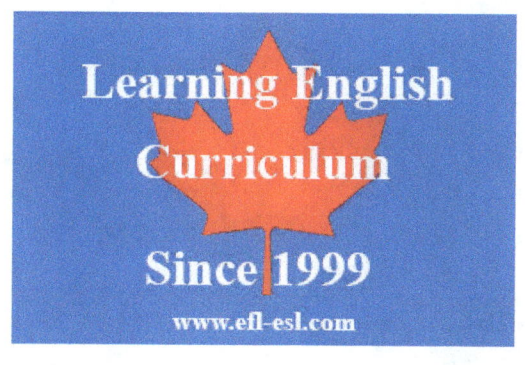

Daisy A. Stocker M.Ed.
George A. Stocker D.D.S.

ESL ANIMALS TEACHER'S GUIDE CONTENTS

		PAGES
Introduction		1-2
Bingo 1	Teacher's Copy	3
Bingo 1	Enrichment Copy	4
Bingo 1	Student Bingo Cards	5-29
Test 1	Student / Answer Pages	30-31
Bingo 2	Teacher Copy	32
Bingo 2	Enrichment Copy	33
Bingo 2	Student Bingo Cards	34-58
Test 2	Student / Answer Pages	59-60
Bingo 3	Teacher's Copy	61
Bingo 3	Enrichment Copy	62
Bingo 3	Student Bingo Cards	63-86
Test 3	Student / Answer Pages	87-88
Bingo 4	Teacher's Copy	89
Bingo 4	Enrichment Copy	90
Bingo 4	Student Bingo Cards	91-115
Final Test 4	Student / Answer Pages	116-121

ESL ANIMALS 1
TEACHER'S GUIDE

CHAPTERS 1 to 12

HOW TO PLAY PICTURE BINGO

Give each student one Bingo Card. For classes with more than 25 students, two or three students can have copies of the same card. It's best if those with identical cards are sitting apart.
The teacher calls the captions listed below in any order. The children are to mark the picture that matches the caption. We suggest that the students use a small object such as a bean or a chestnut.

When they have a horizontal, vertical or diagonal row of pictures with an object in each box, they are to call **BINGO**. The diagonal row must go from corner to corner. The central BINGO box is free.

It is important that the children be allowed to help each other or be given teacher assistance. They should all find the correct picture to match the caption that is called. After playing two or three games they should be encouraged to work independently, although some children will need extra help.

NOTE: The teacher will need to mark the captions as he or she calls and check for mistakes on the papers of the winners

Play calling the Teacher's Captions for many games until the children understand and play without difficulty.

The children use the same cards for the Enrichment Captions. They will learn to use context clues to understand the new words. Play many times.

Student Card sample.

PRIZES: The winners will be delighted with a star or a rubberstamp picture drawn on their exercise book. The same BINGO card can be used for many games by using beans or other small objects. (Dry pasta is good.) Tell the children to keep their cards clean, without marks, so they can play many games. These games motivate the children to learn by listening, understanding and associating the meaning to the picture. They are also learning basic grammar without any formal teaching.

NOTE: The children will be ready for Picture Bingo when they finish Chapter 4.

BINGO 1

**CHAPTERS 1 to 4
TEACHER'S COPY**

Teacher Guide

BINGO 1

CHAPTERS 1 to 4
ENRICHMENT COPY

Teacher Guide

BINGO 1   **CHAPTERS 1 to 4**
CARD 1

Teacher Guide

BINGO 1

CHAPTERS 1 to 4
CARD 2

Teacher Guide

BINGO 1 **CHAPTERS 1 to 4**
CARD 3

Teacher Guide

BINGO 1 **CHAPTERS 1 to 4**
CARD 4

Teacher Guide

8

BINGO 1   **CHAPTERS 1 to 4**
CARD 5

Teacher Guide

BINGO 1

CHAPTERS 1 to 4
CARD 6

Teacher Guide

10

BINGO 1   **CHAPTERS 1 to 4**
                                                                                                                 CARD 7

Teacher Guide

BINGO 1

CHAPTERS 1 to 4
CARD 8

Teacher Guide

12

BINGO 1

CHAPTERS 1 to 4
CARD 9

Teacher Guide

BINGO 1

CHAPTERS 1 to 4
CARD 10

Bb	Cc	(duck)	(red crayon)	(blue crayon)
(sailboat)	1	(puppy)	Aa	(pumpkin)
4	3	BINGO	(ball)	(crayons)
(two children)	Dd	(alligator)	(car)	(clown)
2	(cat)	(panda)	(dinosaur)	(doll)

Teacher Guide

14

BINGO 1

CHAPTERS 1 to 4
CARD 11

Teacher Guide

BINGO 1

CHAPTERS 1 to 4
CARD 12

Teacher Guide

16

BINGO 1

CHAPTERS 1 to 4
CARD 13

Teacher Guide

17

BINGO 1

CHAPTERS 1 to 4
CARD 14

Teacher Guide

BINGO 1   **CHAPTERS 1 to 4**
                                               CARD 15

BINGO

Teacher Guide

BINGO 1

CHAPTERS 1 to 4
CARD 16

Teacher Guide

THE ALPHABET STORY FROM A to L
BINGO 1

CHAPTERS 1 to 4
CARD 17

Teacher Guide

21

BINGO 1

CHAPTERS 1 to 4
CARD 18

Teacher Guide

BINGO 1

CHAPTERS 1 to 4
CARD 19

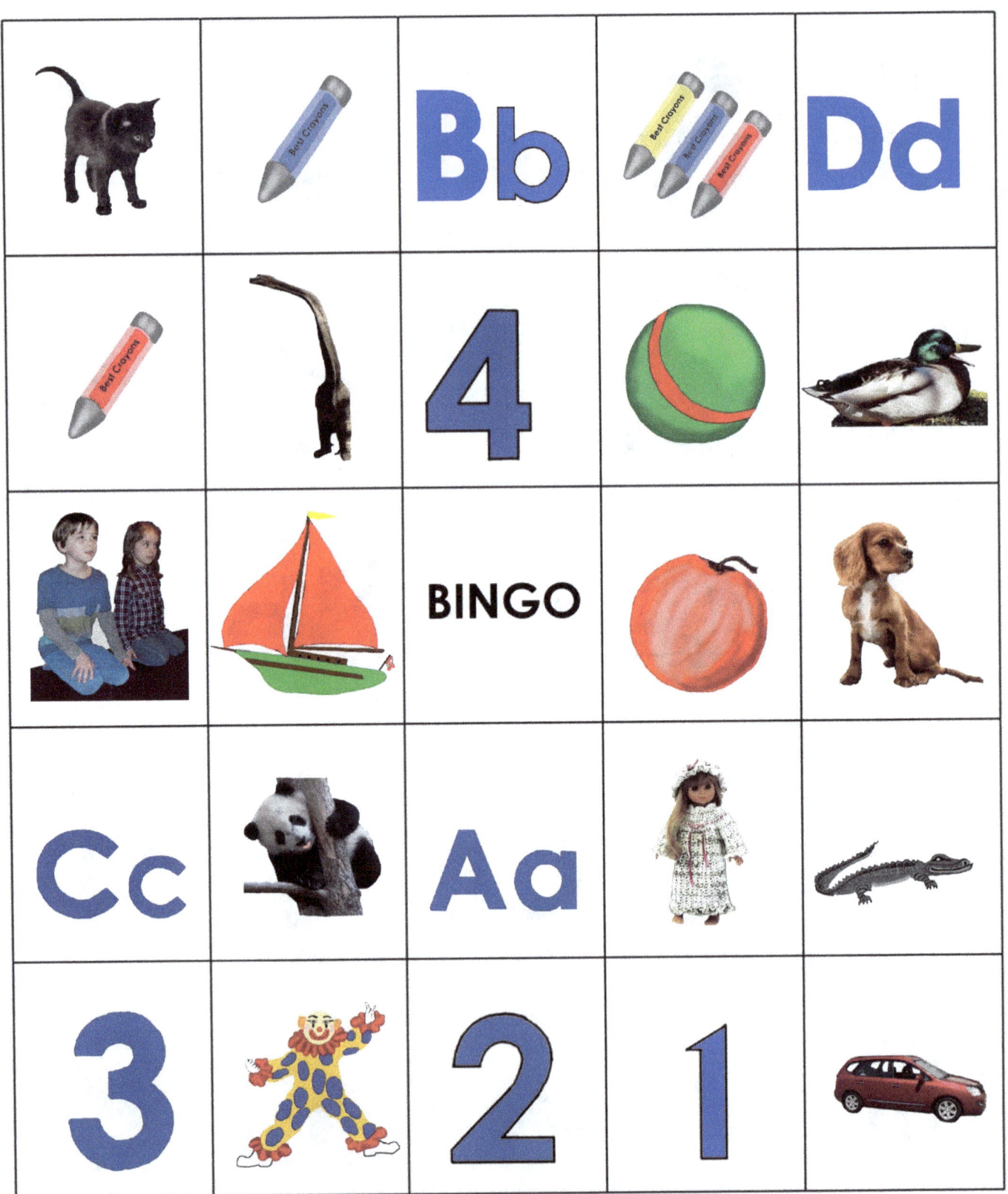

Teacher Guide

BINGO 1

CHAPTERS 1 to 4
CARD 20

Teacher Guide

24

BINGO 1

CHAPTERS 1 to 4
CARD 21

Teacher Guide

BINGO 1

CHAPTERS 1 to 4
CARD 22

Teacher Guide

26

BINGO 1

CHAPTERS 1 to 4
CARD 23

Teacher Guide

BINGO 1

CHAPTERS 1 to 4
CARD 24

Teacher Guide

BINGO 1   **CHAPTERS 1 to 4**
CARD 25

Teacher Guide

TEST 1   CHAPTERS 1- 4

NAME: _____

   Dd

   Aa

   Cc

   Bb

4

3

Have the children point to each picture and say its name then point to the crayons and say "crayons 3", "dolls 4".

They are to draw a line from each picture to its first letter – each number picture and its numeral.

Give 1 mark for each correct line for a total of 10 marks. If the children have a score of less than 8, go back and review as necessary.

Teacher Guide

TEST 1   ANSWERS

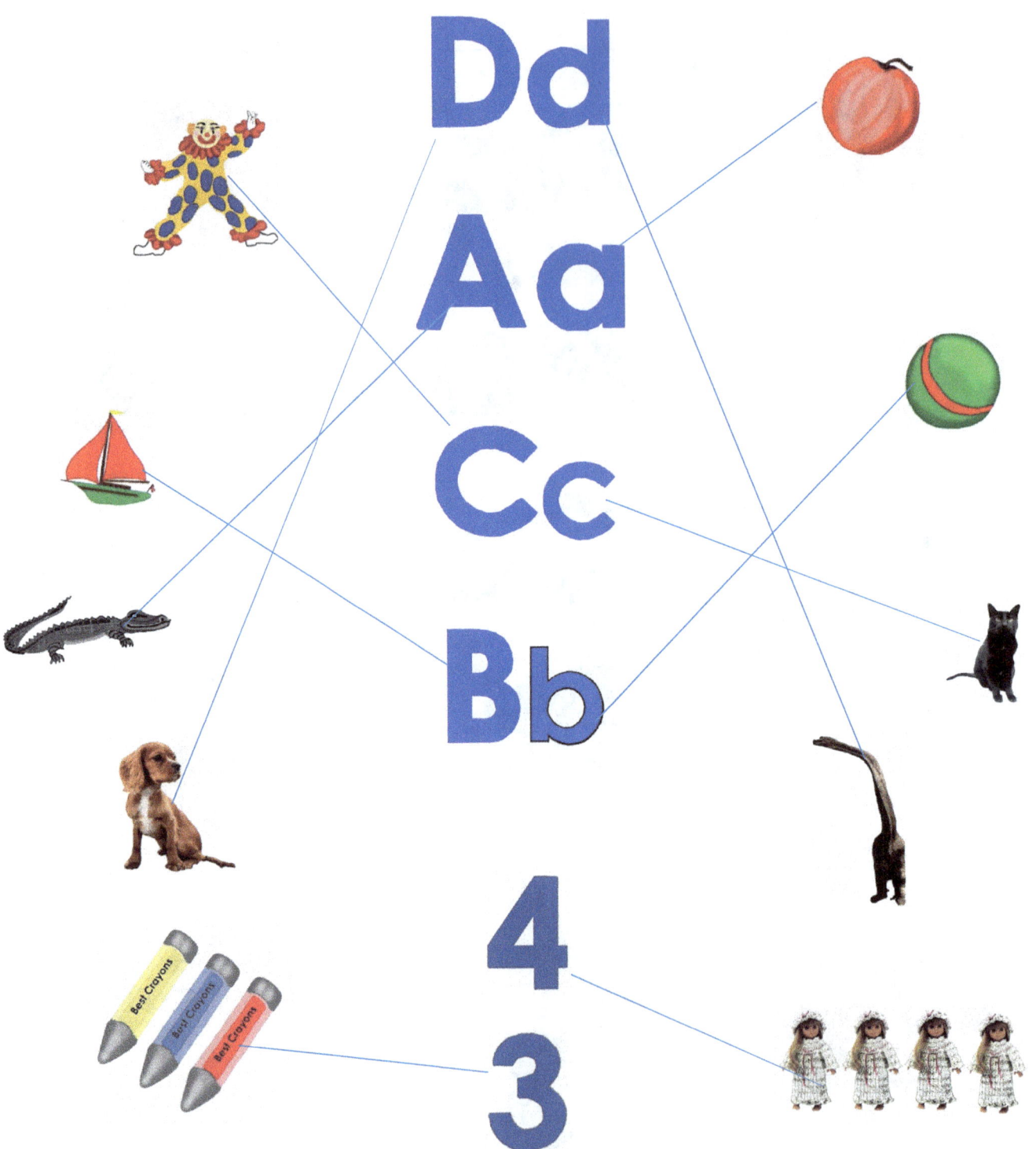

Have the children point to each picture and say its name then point to the crayons and say "crayon 3", "dolls 4".

They are to draw a line from each picture to its first letter – each number picture and its numeral.

Give 1 mark for each correct line for a total of 10 marks. If the children have a score of less than 8, go back and review as necessary. Answers are included for your convenience in the event that you have another student mark the papers.

Teacher Guide

BINGO 2

CHAPTERS 5 to 8
TEACHER'S COPY

BINGO 2

CHAPTERS 5 to 8
ENRICHMENT COPY

Teacher Guide

BINGO 2

CHAPTERS 5 to 8
CARD 1

Teacher Guide

34

BINGO 2

CHAPTERS 5 to 8
CARD 2

Teacher Guide

BINGO 2   **CHAPTERS 5 to 8**
CARD 3

Teacher Guide

BINGO 2

CHAPTERS 5 to 8
CARD 4

Teacher Guide

BINGO 2 CHAPTERS 5 to 8
CARD 5

Teacher Guide

BINGO 2

CHAPTERS 5 to 8
CARD 6

Teacher Guide

BINGO 2

CHAPTERS 5 to 8
CARD 7

Teacher Guide

40

BINGO 2

CHAPTERS 5 to 8
CARD 8

Teacher Guide

BINGO 2

CHAPTERS 5 to 8
CARD 9

Teacher Guide

42

BINGO 2

CHAPTERS 5 to 8
CARD 10

Teacher Guide

BINGO 2

CHAPTERS 5 to 8
CARD 11

Teacher Guide

44

BINGO 2

CHAPTERS 5 to 8
CARD 12

Teacher Guide

BINGO 2

CHAPTERS 5 to 8
CARD 13

Teacher Guide

46

BINGO 2   **CHAPTERS 5 to 8**
CARD 14

Ff	8			
5	Gg			
		BINGO		
6		7	Hh	
Ee				

Teacher Guide

BINGO 2

CHAPTERS 5 to 8
CARD 15

Teacher Guide

BINGO 2

CHAPTERS 5 to 8
CARD 16

Teacher Guide

49

BINGO 2

CHAPTERS 5 to 8
CARD 17

Teacher Guide

BINGO 2

CHAPTERS 5 to 8
CARD 18

Teacher Guide

51

BINGO 2

CHAPTERS 5 to 8
CARD 19

Teacher Guide

52

BINGO 2 **CHAPTERS 5 to 8**
CARD 20

Teacher Guide

53

BINGO 2

CHAPTERS 5 to 8
CARD 21

Teacher Guide

54

BINGO 2   CHAPTERS 5 to 8
CARD 22

Teacher Guide

BINGO 2

CHAPTERS 5 to 8
CARD 23

Teacher Guide

56

BINGO 2

CHAPTERS 5 to 8
CARD 24

Teacher Guide

BINGO 2

CHAPTERS 5 to 8
CARD 25

Teacher Guide

TEST 2 **CHAPTERS 5 to 8**

NAME: _____

7
5
8
6

Cc
Ee
Hh
Gg
Ff
Dd

Have the children point to each picture and say its name

They are to draw a line from each number to the picture it represents.

Next, they are to draw a line from each letter to the picture with that first sound.

Give 1 mark for each correct line for a total of 10 marks. If the children have a score of less than 8, go back and review as necessary.

Teacher Guide

TEST 2 ANSWERS

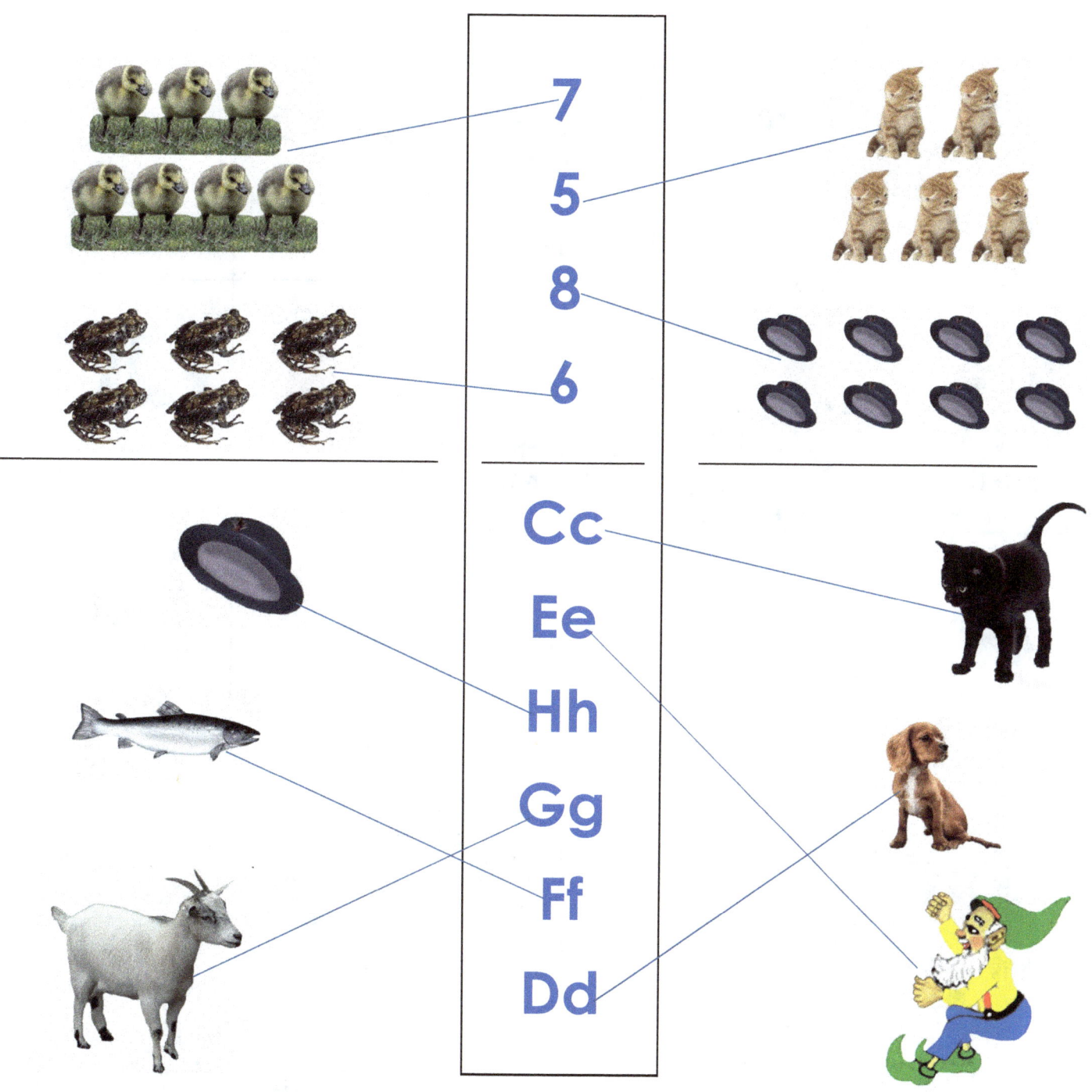

Have the children point to each picture and say its name

They are to draw a line from each number to the picture it represents.

Next they are to draw a line from each letter to the picture with that first sound.

Give 1 mark for each correct line for a total of 10 marks. If the children have a score of less than 8, go back and review as necessary. Answers are included for your convenience in the event that you have another student mark the papers.

Teacher Guide

REVIEW: BINGO 3

CHAPTERS 1 to 8
TEACHER'S COPY

 This letter's name is Gg.	 This bird is flying.	 It is the letter Aa.	 It's a big fish.	 It's a dangerous dinosaur!
 This little dog is friendly.	 The horse stands in the hay.	 Gg is the first sound in this animal's name.	 It's a big red apple.	 This letter's name is Dd.
 It's a mother goose and gosling.	 George catches a fish.	BINGO	 This letter's name is Ff.	 Cc is the first sound in this animal's name.
 It is the letter Bb.	 There are two geese.	 Ee is the first sound in this animal's name.	 George is in the hay.	 C is the first letter in Cassie.
 It is the first letter in horse.	 Elizabeth runs.	 The ball is green and red.	 It is the first letter in elf.	 This horse is eating grass.

Teacher Guide

REVIEW: BINGO 3

CHAPTERS 1 to 8
ENRICHMENT COPY

 This letter is the first sound in goat.	 It's a bird in the sky.	 This letter is the first sound in alligator.	 This is a big fish.	 The dinosaur has a very long neck.
 The little dog is a puppy.	 The horse's legs are in the hay.	 This animal has horns on its head.	 It grows on a tree.	 This letter is the first sound in duck.
 The mother goose has one gosling.	 George is fishing in a pond.	BINGO	 It is the first sound in frog.	 This animal is black.
 This is the first sound in boat.	 There is a goose and a gander.	 This animal has a long trunk.	 George shouts!	 It is the first letter in cat.
 It is the first sound in hat.	 Elizabeth has a red blouse.	 It is green with a red stripe.	 It is the first sound in Elizabeth.	 You can see the horse's long tail.

Teacher Guide

REVIEW: BINGO 3   **CHAPTERS 1 to 8 — CARD 1**

Gg		Aa		
				Dd
		BINGO	Ff	
Bb				Cc
Hh			Ee	

Teacher Guide

REVIEW: **CHAPTERS 1 to 8**

BINGO 3   **CARD 2**

Teacher Guide

REVIEW: BINGO 3

CHAPTERS 1 to 8
CARD 3

Teacher Guide

65

REVIEW: BINGO 3

CHAPTERS 1 to 8
CARD 4

Teacher Guide

66

REVIEW: BINGO 3

CHAPTERS 1 to 8
CARD 5

Teacher Guide

67

REVIEW: BINGO 3

CHAPTERS 1 to 8
CARD 6

Dd	Cc	 (orange)	 (goose)	Bb
(elephant)	Ff	(monkey)	(fishing)	(eagle)
(ball)	(geese)	BINGO	Aa	(horse)
Hh	(dog)	(cat)	(child)	Gg
(goat)	(fish)	(horse)	Ee	(girl)

Teacher Guide

68

REVIEW: BINGO 3

CHAPTERS 1 to 8
CARD 7

	Cc			Bb
	Ff	Hh		
	Dd	BINGO	Aa	Ee
				Gg

Teacher Guide

69

REVIEW: BINGO 3

CHAPTERS 1 to 8
CARD 8

Teacher Guide

70

REVIEW: BINGO 3

CHAPTERS 1 to 8
CARD 9

Teacher Guide

71

REVIEW: BINGO 3

CHAPTERS 1 to 8
CARD 10

Teacher Guide

72

REVIEW: **CHAPTERS 1 to 8**

              BINGO 3   **CARD 11**

Teacher Guide

REVIEW: BINGO 3

CHAPTERS 1 to 8
CARD 12

Teacher Guide

74

REVIEW: BINGO 3

CHAPTERS 1 to 8
CARD 13

Teacher Guide

75

REVIEW: BINGO 3

CHAPTERS 1 to 8
CARD 14

Teacher Guide

REVIEW: BINGO 3

**CHAPTERS 1 to 8
CARD 16**

Teacher Guide

REVIEW: BINGO 3 CARD 17

Teacher Guide

78

REVIEW: BINGO 3 CARD 18

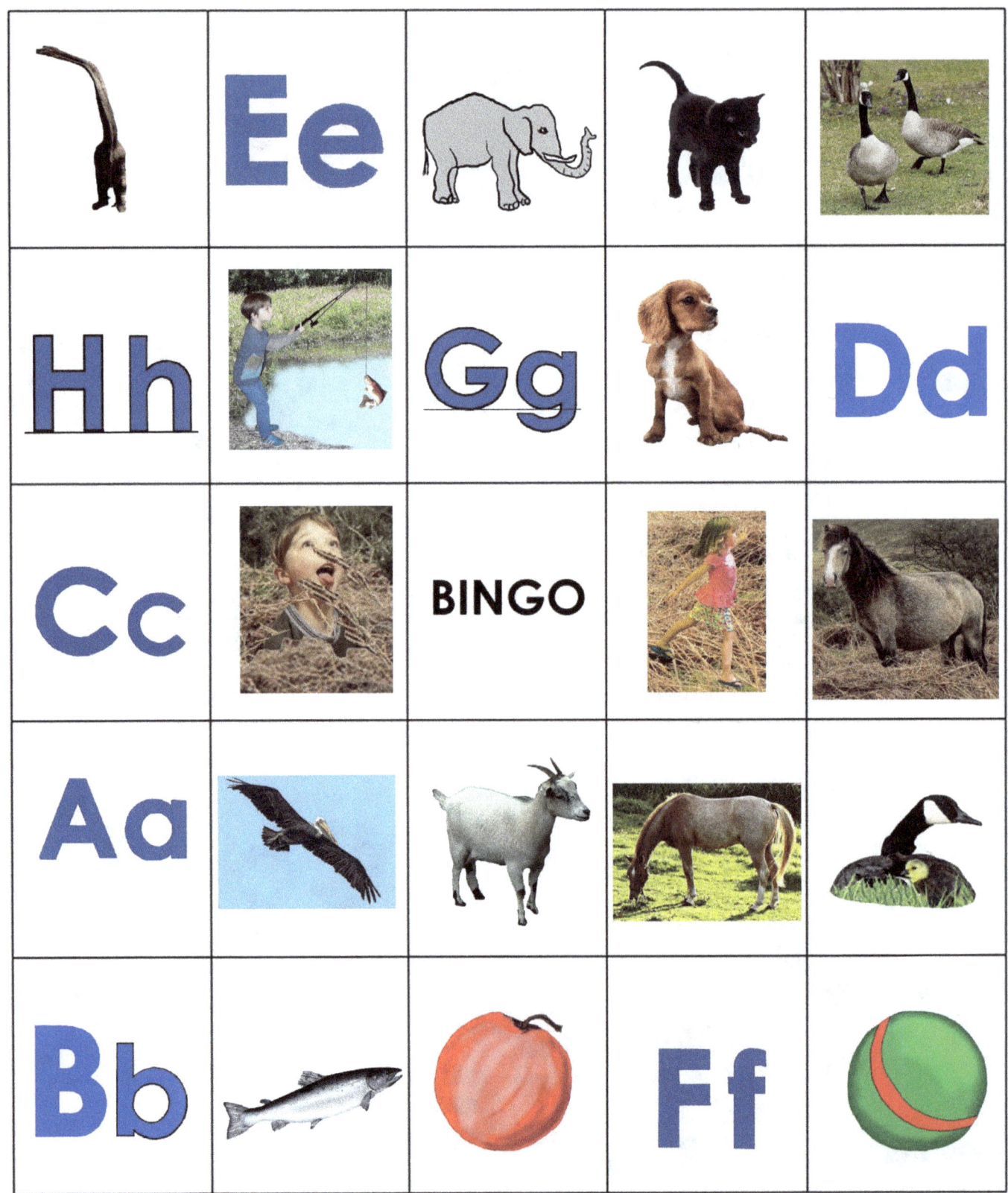

Teacher Guide

REVIEW: BINGO 3 CARD 19

Teacher Guide

80

REVIEW: BINGO 3 CARD 20

Teacher Guide

81

REVIEW: BINGO 3 CARD 21

Teacher Guide

82

REVIEW: BINGO 3 CARD 22

Teacher Guide

83

REVIEW: BINGO 3 CARD 23

Teacher Guide

84

REVIEW: BINGO 3 CARD 24

Teacher Guide

85

REVIEW: BINGO 3 CARD 25

TEST 3: PAGE 1

NAME: _____

gander

frog

doll

_____

Hh

Ii

Gg

Jj

_____

8

9

10

We suggest that this test be used to assess the needs of the students and to give them encouragement with their success.

It is important that the test is given according to the instructions on Page 88.

Answers are included for your convenience in the event that you have another student mark the papers.

TEST 3: ANSWERS

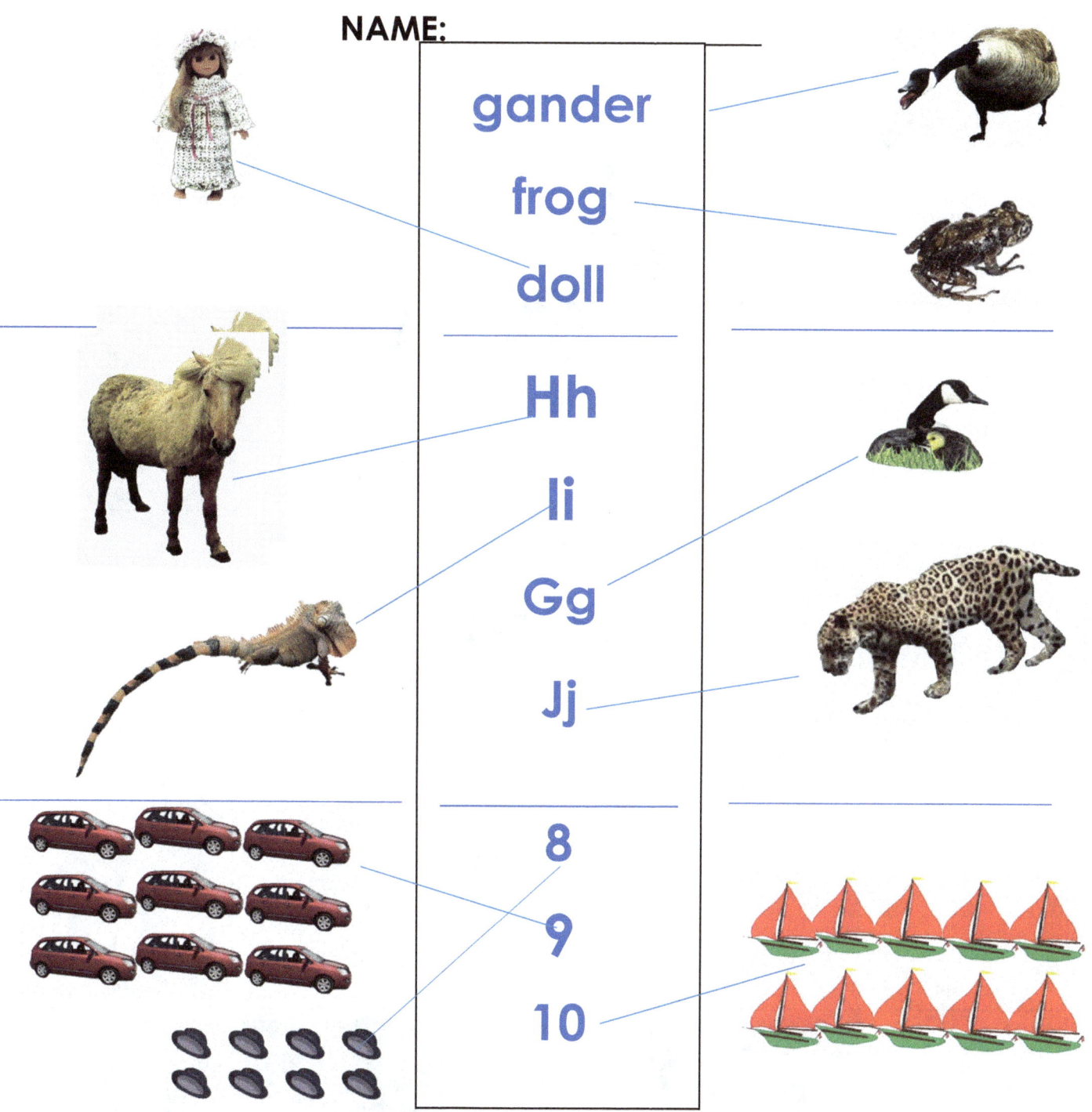

Important: It is important that the children start at the top, with the words, as there are several pictures with the same letter.

First Instructions: The children are to draw a line from each word to the picture it describes.

Second Instruction: When they are ready, they are to draw a line from each letter to the picture with that first sound.

Third Instructions: When they are ready, they are to draw a line from the number to the appropriate picture. **(1 mark each)**

Teacher Guide

BINGO 4

**CHAPTERS 9 to 12
TEACHER'S COPY**

Teacher Guide

BINGO 4

CHAPTERS 9 to 12
ENRICHMENT COPY

Teacher Guide

90

BINGO 4 CHAPTERS 9 to 12
CARD 1

	i		k	11
		9	10	
12		BINGO		j
	K		J	
		L		

Teacher Guide

BINGO 4 **CHAPTERS 9 to 12**
CARD 2

BINGO 4

CHAPTERS 9 to 12
CARD 3

9			10	11
k			i	L
12		BINGO		j
		C	J	
		K		

Teacher Guide

93

BINGO 4

CHAPTERS 9 to 12
CARD 4

BINGO 4

CHAPTERS 9 to 12
CARD 5

Teacher Guide

95

BINGO 4 **CHAPTERS 9 to 12**
CARD 6

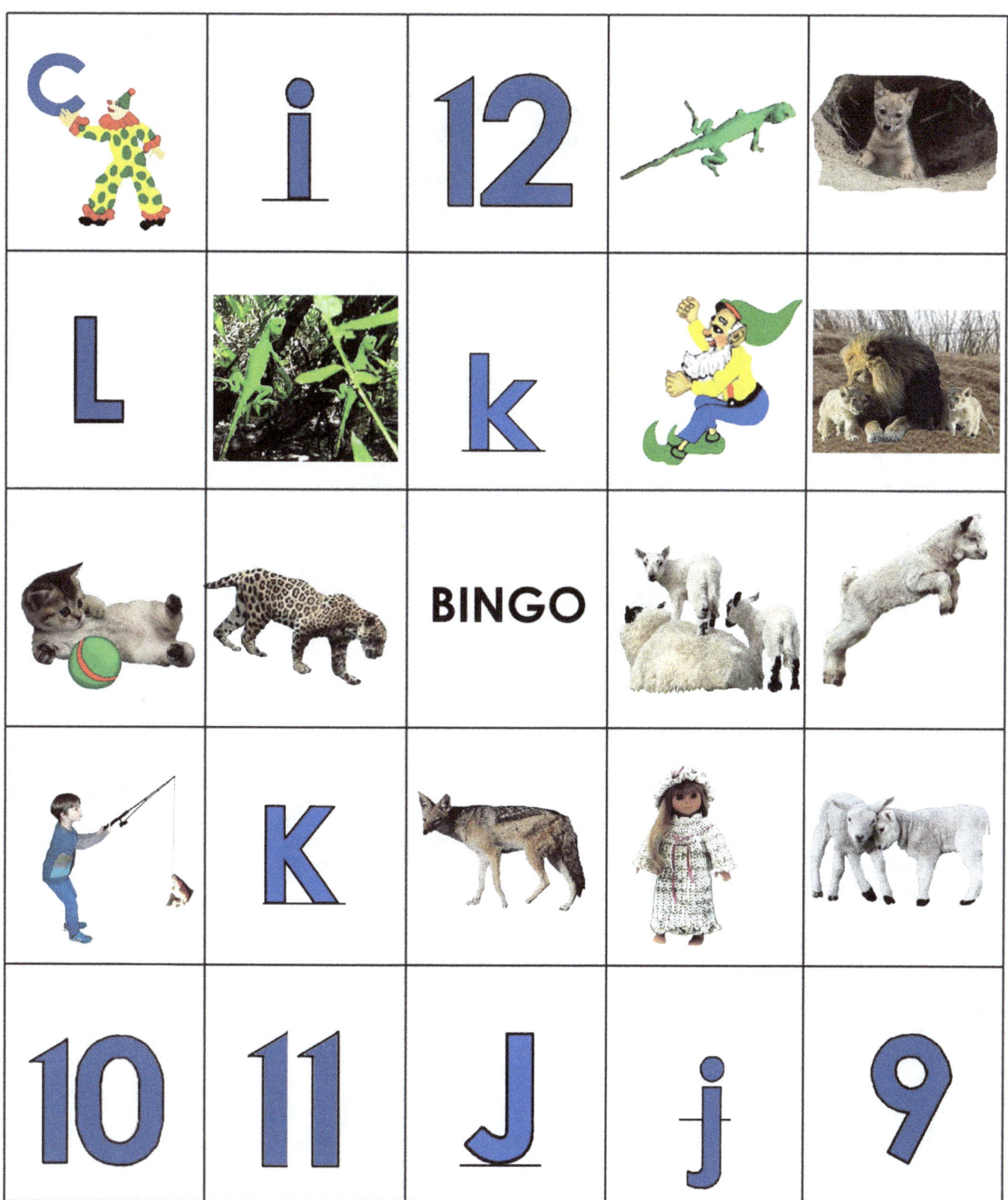

Teacher Guide

BINGO 4

CHAPTERS 9 to 12
CARD 7

🦎	9	🐱	10	🐐
11	k	🧝	🐆	🎣
j	🦁	BINGO	🐑	i
L	🐑	🐺	J	👧
🦎	🦊	K	12	🤡 C

Teacher Guide

97

BINGO 4   **CHAPTERS 9 to 12**
                               CARD 8

Teacher Guide

98

BINGO 4   **CHAPTERS 9 to 12**
CARD 9

Teacher Guide

BINGO 4 CHAPTERS 9 to 12
CARD 10

Teacher Guide

100

BINGO 4

CHAPTERS 9 to 12
CARD 11

Teacher Guide

101

BINGO 4

CHAPTERS 9 to 12
CARD 12

Teacher Guide

102

BINGO 4

CHAPTERS 9 to 12
CARD 13

Teacher Guide

103

BINGO 4   **CHAPTERS 9 to 12**
                                                                CARD 14

Teacher Guide

BINGO 4

CHAPTERS 9 to 12
CARD 15

	i		k	
L	12		11	
		BINGO	K	10
			J	
	j			9

© Learning English with Laughter Ltd.

Teacher Guide

BINGO 4

CHAPTERS 9 to 12
CARD 16

Teacher Guide

106

BINGO 4   **CHAPTERS 9 to 12**
CARD 17

9	i			11
K	j			k
		BINGO		12
			J	
	L	10		C

Teacher Guide

BINGO 4

CHAPTERS 9 to 12
CARD 18

Teacher Guide

108

BINGO 4

CHAPTERS 9 to 12
CARD 19

12			C	J
k				K
		BINGO	i	
11		L		10
j		9		

Teacher Guide

BINGO 4

CHAPTERS 9 to 12
CARD 20

	i	10	12	
9		k		
L		BINGO		
		11	K	
		J	j	

Teacher Guide

110

BINGO 4

CHAPTERS 9 to 12
CARD 21

Teacher Guide

BINGO 4

CHAPTERS 9 to 12
CARD 22

Teacher Guide

BINGO 4

CHAPTERS 9 to 12
CARD 23

Teacher Guide

113

BINGO 4

CHAPTERS 9 to 12
CARD 24

j	c	10		11
J			i	
	k	BINGO		
	L		12	
9				K

Teacher Guide

114

BINGO 4

CHAPTERS 9 to 12
CARD 25

	i		j	10
			K	9
		BINGO		
	k	12	J	
	L	11		

Teacher Guide

FINAL TEST 4: PAGE 1

Name: _____

Aa

Bb

Gg

Dd

Ii

Jj

Hh

Ll

Cc

Ee

Have the children point to each picture as you say its name:
dog, bird, iguana, goat, alligator, jaguar, lambs, cat, elephant, horse.

The students are to draw a line from each picture to the letter of its first sound. (**1 mark each.**)

Review any areas of difficulty before moving to the next book: ESL ANIMALS M to Z.

Teacher Guide

FINAL TEST 4: PAGE 2

Name: _____

9

7

3

6

11

5

12

10

8

4

Have the children point to each picture and name the objects:
goslings, crayons, cars, balls, clowns, frogs, kittens, elephants, hats, boats,

Explain: They are to count the number of objects in each picture and draw a line from the picture to the number. (**1 mark each.**)

Teacher Guide

117

FINAL TEST 4: PAGE 3

Name: _____

The mother goose has a gosling.

The cat is fishing.

The elf sits on the elephant.

The two lambs are friendly.

It's a dangerous jaguar!

Note: This page asks the children to associate the text with some new pictures. It may challenge some students.

The children are to read the captions and draw a line to the picture they describe. **(1 mark each.)**

There is a total of 25 marks. Answers are included for your convenience in the event that you have another student mark the papers.

Teacher Guide

118

FINAL TEST 4:   ANSWERS

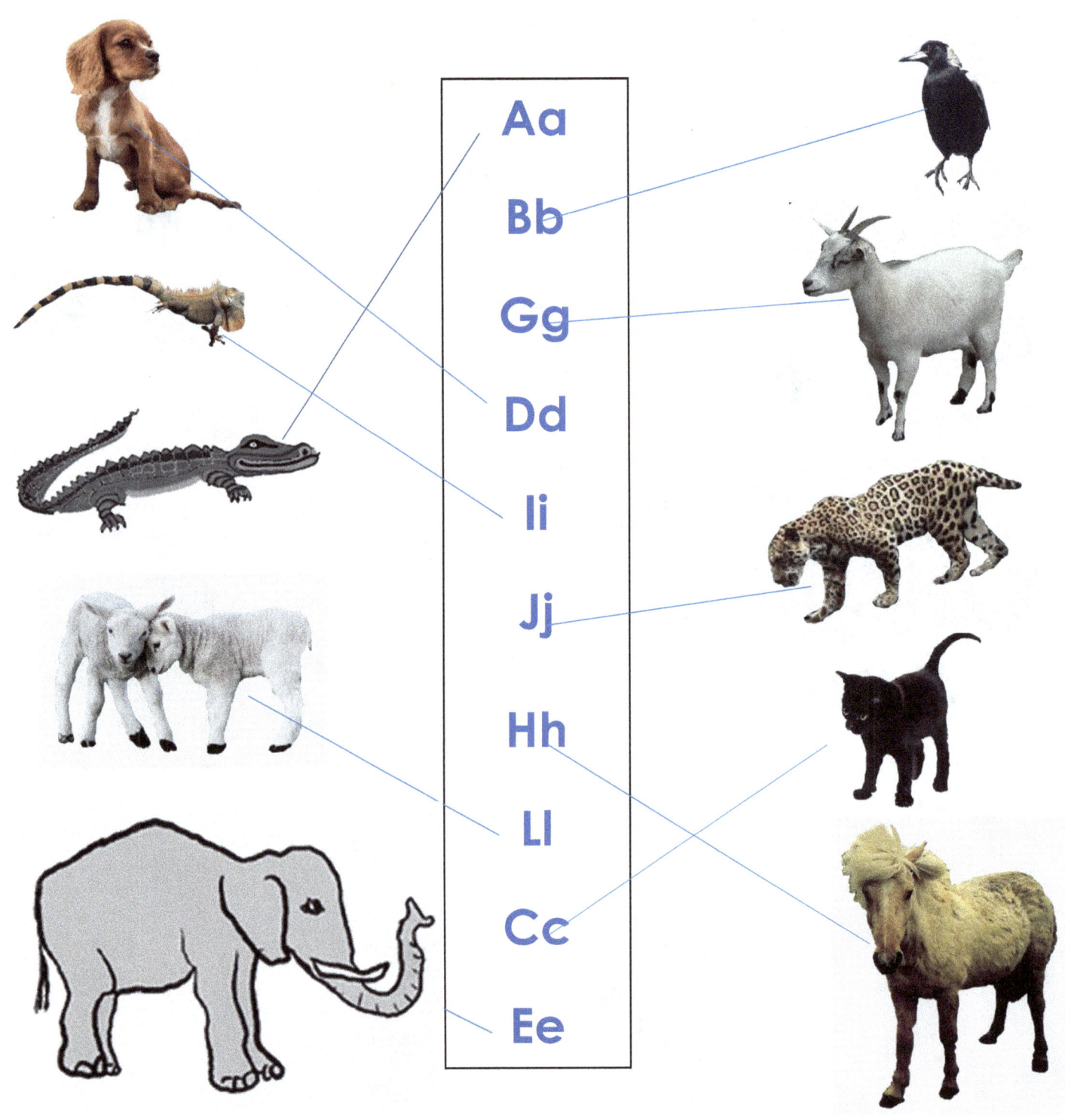

Have the children point to each picture as you say its name:
dog, bird, iguana, goat, alligator, jaguar, lambs, cat, elephant, horse.
The students are to draw a line from each picture to the letter of its first sound. (**1 mark each.**) Review any areas of difficulty before moving to the next book: ESL ANIMALS M to Z.

Teacher Guide

TEST 4: ANSWERS

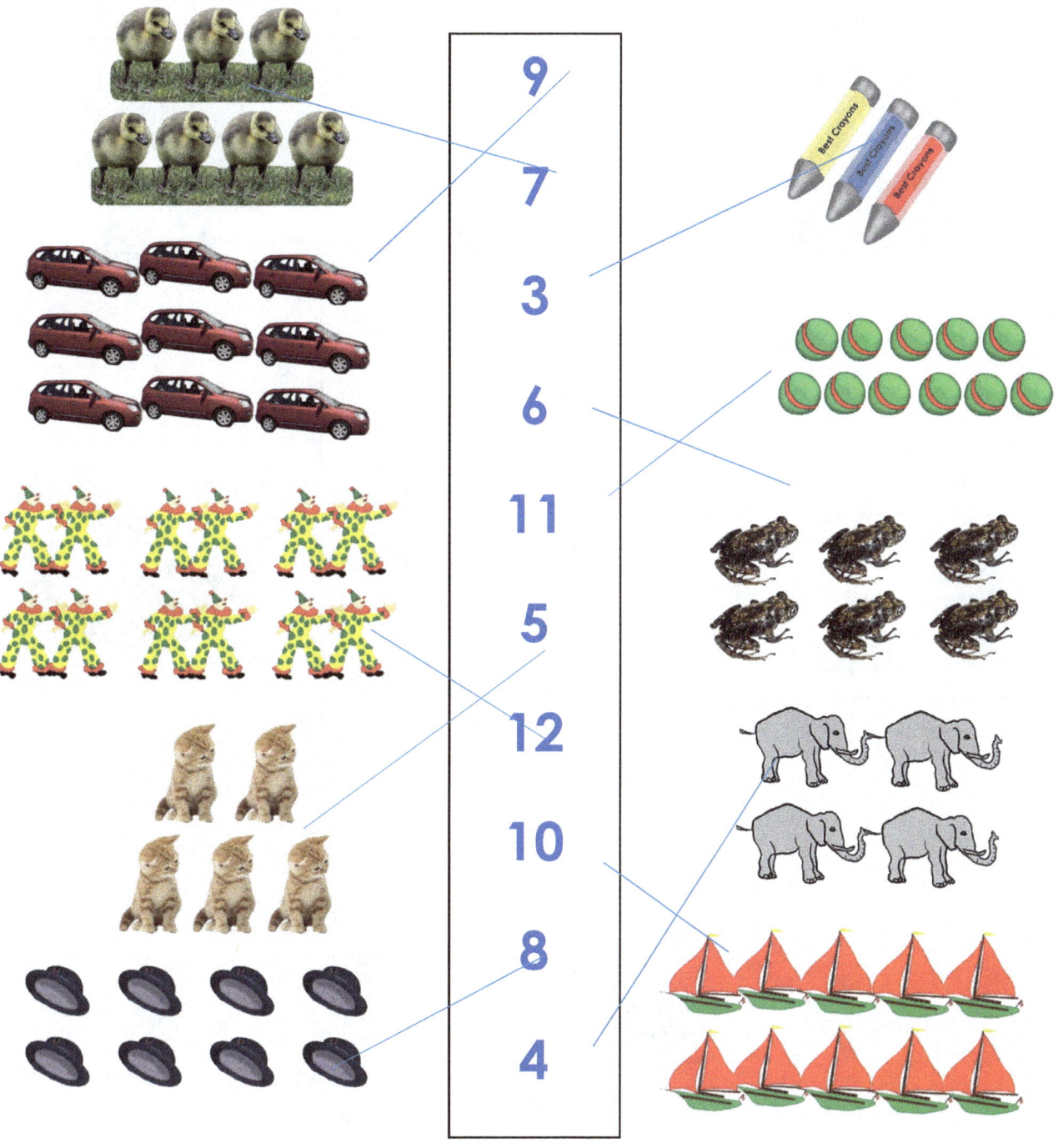

Have the children point to each picture and name the objects:
goslings, crayons, cars, balls, clowns, frogs, kittens, elephants, hats, boats,

(1 mark each.)

Teacher Guide

TEST 4: ANSWERS

The mother goose has a gosling.

The cat is fishing.

The elf sits on the elephant.

The two lambs are friendly.

It's a dangerous jaguar!

Note: This page asks the children to associate the text with some new pictures. It may challenge some students.
(1 mark each.) There is a total of 25 marks.
Answers are included for your convenience in the event that you have another student mark the papers.

Teacher Guide

Visit us Online for More

https://www.efl-esl.com

Listening and Speaking Workbook

Complete Listening and Speaking English Workbook – includes full downloadable audio!

- Vocabulary for each Lesson
- Everyday Conversations – Listen to full audio then role-play!
- 14 Lessons
- 2 Review Chapters
- 2 Full Audio Tests with Answer Key
- Role Play
- Telephone Conversations and role play
- Question and Answer Dialogues

https://efl-esl.com/listening-speaking-english/

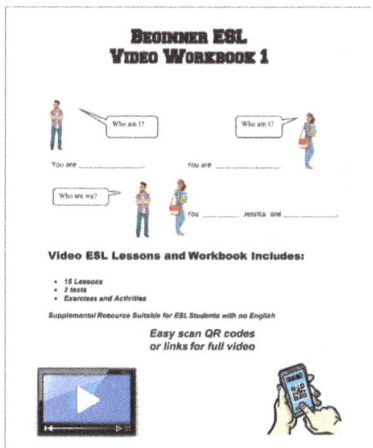

Beginners ESL Video Workbook

Includes:

- 15 lesson plans with full video
- Supplemental activities and games
- Video introduction for all topics

Learn More https://efl-esl.com/video-workbooks/

ESL Graphic Novels for Kids (Comic Books)

These books offer an oral approach for young ESL / EFL students aged 6 - 10.

They contain high interest stories, written in the graphics novel format that children love. This is very suitable for supplementary study, home school, as well as for summer camps.

https://efl-esl.com/esl-graphic-novels-for-children/

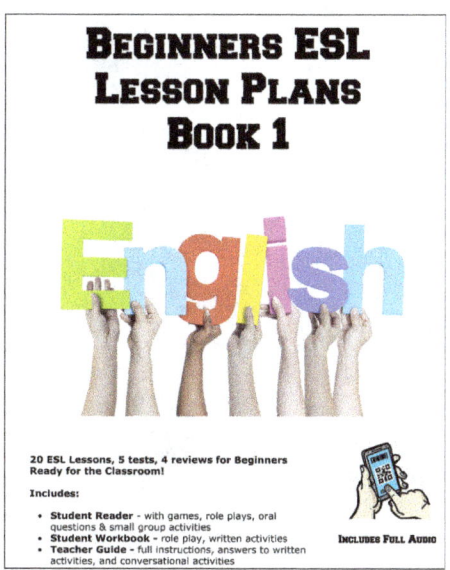

https://efl-esl.com/curriculum/module-1/

20 Beginners ESL Lesson Plans with full audio - Ready for the Classroom

Includes full audio, student reader, student workbook and complete teacher guide!

Our curriculum is used in over 100 countries since 2005

Includes:

- 5 tests, 4 reviews
- **Student Reader** - with games, role plays, oral questions & small group activities
- **Student Workbook** - role play, written activities
- **Teacher Guide** - full instructions, answers to written activities, and conversational activities

Fun and Engaging Conversational Activities and Role Plays like:

- Greetings
- Introductions
- The family
- Taking to classmates and friends

Activities and Games include

- Oral questions
- Small group asking and answering questions then checking the answers provided
- Role-plays
- Picture Bingo
- Memory games
- Greetings
- Asking for addresses and nationalities
- Word Bingo

www.ingramcontent.com/pod-product-compliance
Lightning Source LLC
Chambersburg PA
CBHW080339170426
43194CB00014B/2619